Forests, Wild And Cultivated

Augustine Henry

XI.

FORESTS, WILD AND CULTIVATED.[1]

By AUGUSTINE HENRY, M.A., F.L.S., L.R.C.P. (Ed.).

PLATES IX.–XX.

I. WILD FORESTS.

MAN, since he emerged from the purely hunting stage, has been at work destroying the natural forest. The primitive modes of this destruction may still be observed in countries like China, where in the south, for example, the Yaos, a semi-hunting tribe, who always live in isolated villages, on the margins of virgin forests in the high mountains, cut the trees around them, as out of the bamboos, which form the dense underwood, they manufacture paper, and in clearings they cultivate certain drug-plants and indigo. Other tribes indulge in what I term nomadic agriculture; they burn down areas of the forest; gather one or two crops of millet or upland rice from the rich forest soil; and then pass on to another district, where they repeat the destruction. With people in a higher stage of civilization, forest clearings are effected more rapidly; and all the good land, which was generally covered primitively with trees, becomes the seat of agriculture and pasture. In addition, there are vast demands made upon the forest for fuel; and in most countries, primitive iron works have been, perhaps, the chief cause of the destruction of vast forest regions.

In our own country the destruction of the forests is well-nigh complete. Nearly every bog is the site of an ancient forest. It appears to be an almost constant rule that, once forests are cut down by man, it is with great difficulty they are naturally reproduced. In warmer countries, desert- or grass-land is now found where ancient forests stood; and in the northern temperate zone,

---

[1] Lecture given before the Royal Dublin Society, February 5, 1904.

the invasion of heather and production of peat-mosses constantly
occur where the climate is moist.   The heather, a social plant, will
not grow under the shade of trees; but when these are cut down,
it invades the felled area, and it may be supposed to poison the
soil, for only a few trees will grow on heaths, and scarcely any on
bogs.   At any rate, regeneration is always difficult in such situations, and is impossible where cattle have access.   Little can be
alleged against the utilization of good soils for farming or grazing;
but in most parts of the world there are immense areas, once clad
with trees, which are now covered by coarse grasses, or are semi-
deserts, or heaths, or bogs; and all such cases are economically
disastrous.   Waste lands, unsuitable for farm crops, or useless as
pasture, are the results of man's ancient ruinous agency; and on
the Continent it is now accepted as an axiom that such areas should
be, where possible, re-afforested.

Plate IX., fig. 1, represents a hill in central China, covered
with coarse grass, useless as pasture, and impossible to cultivate.
In such regions farming is carried on only in the rich land of the
valleys.   Plate IX., fig. 2, shows a Yao village in the Shan States,
where the primitive people are making the first onslaught on the
primeval forest.   Plate X., fig. 1, depicts the remains of an
ancient forest in Donegal, near Mount Errigal.

In Europe, primeval forest only remains in a few isolated districts.   In Ireland, an oak forest, a mile square, in a virgin
condition, exists still on the Clonbrock estate; and at Killarney
there is the remarkable association of arbutus and oak, which constitutes a type of forest quite unique, as here the arbutus reaches
the dimensions of a forest tree, and, mixed with the oak, keeps
possession of a considerable area of rocky soil.   In France and
southern Europe generally, the arbutus is only a shrub.   In our
glens, here and there little bits of ancient forest remain; and
Mr. Welch, of Belfast, informs me that in such woods peculiar
land shells occur, which are never found where the soil has been
disturbed by cultivation.

It is difficult, now-a-days, from the paucity of true virgin
forests, to study the primitive condition of the earth's surface,
upon which man has been such a disturbing agent.   We know
that a contest is continually going on between the wood-land

and the grass-land ; and while generally the success of one or other depends upon climatic factors, yet I believe no adequate explanation has been given of the general phenomenon that, where forests are destroyed by man, grass-land takes the upper hand.

It is, however, possible to give a fairly adequate account of the garment of the earth in ancient times, before man had begun to exercise his disturbing influence. In that epoch the earth was covered either with large tracts of grass, or with wood-land, or—in regions subject to drought or extreme dry cold— it was desert. A desert is a territory where individual plants are separated by wide intervals of sand or rock. It is rare for a desert to be entirely devoid of plants, as even the Sahara has a flora. In the popular imagination deserts are only associated with hot regions; but two other types occur. There are the tundras, which occur in the northern partsof Russia, Siberia, and North America, where such plants as occur are isolated, stunted in form, and mostly of low organisation, as mosses and lichens; and the Alpine deserts which occur in the Himalayas between the grass-land and the snow-line.

In the regions free from desert, either grass-land or wood-land prevailed; and the occurrence of one or other depended entirely upon climate. A grass-land is covered with perennial grasses, growing in tufts and intermingled with many kinds of herbs. Grasses are shallow-rooting plants, and as such are dependent for their existence upon the continuous presence of moisture in the superficial layers of the soil during the vegetative season. The uppermost layer of the soil speedily dries up; and grass-land is only possible when there are frequent rains in spring and summer. Trees, unlike grasses, are deep-rooting plants. By their spreading network of roots they tap deep-lying sources of water. Trees will accordingly grow if the deeper parts of the subsoil contain water, and it does not practically matter, provided the annual rainfall is large, at what season the rain falls. Trees occur in regions like the shores of the Mediterranean, where there are long seasons of drought. The greater the amount of moisture in the subsoil, the taller will be the trees, and the more luxurious their growth. As trees transpire moisture in enormous quantity, calmness of the air helps their growth, as winds cause excess of transpiration ; and in frosty weather, when water cannot be taken up from the soil by trees, dry winds will kill them. In extreme Arctic regions trees are not found, simply on account of the cold drying winds of the Arctic winter. It is not the low temperature in itself which stops tree-growth, for the coldest part of the earth's surface is in the Siberian forest district.

In mountains, to a considerable altitude, there is a heavier rainfall than in the adjoining plain, so that the subsoil is kept continuously wet. As a result, the slopes of mountains are commonly covered with forests. Higher still, on lofty mountains, the rainfall diminishes, and strong winds prevail; and, in consequence, we find above the timber-line the Alpine grass-land, which in Europe extends up to the snow-line.

A good wood-land climate consists, then, of the following elements:—A warm season of growth, a continuously wet subsoil (heavy rainfall), and calm, damp air, especially in winter. Climate is thus the important factor. Soil only exerts a modifying influence. Heaths cover large tracts in Europe; and they probably owe their existence to the poverty of the soil, which satisfies the wants of the common heather, but is inadequate to the requirements of trees, or is even poisonous to them. In Norfolk, the heaths, however, if enclosed against cattle, are rapidly repeopled by the common pine, provided the subsoil is porous sand containing water; and the conversion of heath-land into wood-land is easy in many districts with slight aid from man. Near bodies of water the subsoil remains moist to a considerable depth, and this is why the margins of rivers and lakes are covered with woods. These "fringing forests" are often of considerable importance, and may be as luxuriant as forests in the best forest climate. The swamp forests of Florida, and the mangrove forests which fringe the sea-coasts in the tropics, are peculiar communities, which are due to special soil-conditions. The occurrence of rocks will prevent the growth of either trees or grass; and on them we may find only plants occurring here and there at wide intervals. However, in moist climates, rocks are rapidly weathered, their decomposition being hastened by lowly vegetable organisms: algæ first appear, then mosses and higher plants; and in the end, what were once barren rocks become covered with forests of great luxuriance.

Many splendid forests, as will be alluded to below, occur in the mountains of France in such difficult positions. Plate X., fig. 2, is a picture of the Scalp in County Dublin; one side of the pass is covered by a fine plantation of pine, while the other side is a semi-desert, with scattered grass and whins occurring here and there amidst the rocks. On the precipice of the Scalp, next the pine plantation (see Plate XI., fig. 1), trees may be seen taking possession of a rocky and barren situation. The leaves blown over from the plantation have collected in crevices, and have formed, by their decay, pockets of humus in which seeds have fallen, which are growing up into trees. The Scalp illustrates very well one great advantage of tree-growth, *i.e.* that it actually creates soil, and always improves its fertility. The rocks, rent by the disintegrating action of the roots of the trees, are decomposed by the carbonic acid which is formed abundantly in the humus resulting from the decay of fallen leaves.

There are many types of wood-land on the earth's surface, and I may glance at some of these briefly. In the tropics, in regions where rain falls constantly, the so-called rain-forest prevails, in which the trees are all evergreen. Where wet and dry seasons alternate, there is the monsoon forest, in which many deciduous-leaved trees occur. In still drier regions are the tropical savannah-forests and thorn-forests. In the warmer part of the temperate zones, we have also a rain-forest of evergreen trees: broad-leaved trees in ordinary soil, and conifers where the soil is sandy or swampy. This forest occupies regions where there is an abundant rainfall. In parts where the rainfall is lessened, but where it is still considerable in summer, we have thorn-forests and savannah-forests, including peculiar formations like the eucalyptus and acacia forests of Australia, where the grass grows freely between the trees. In the districts of the warmer belt of the temperate zones, where the climate is characterized by rain in winter and prolonged drought in summer, we have an evergreen xerophilous forest, made up of trees with thick leathery leaves. In the more northerly belt of the north temperate zone, two types of forest occur—the summer forest, composed of deciduous-leaved trees, and the coniferous forest. All these different types are explicable by climate factors alone, slightly modified by conditions of soil.

It is impossible in the limits of a short paper to consider all these types, but one or two may be glanced at. In the tropical rain-forest we are struck by the abundance of epiphytes (plants which live upon trees, like so many orchids and ferns) and of climbers, which everywhere cover the trees. In a tropical forest there are four or five stages—the herbs on the ground ; above these a tier of shrubs; and still higher, two or three tiers of trees attaining different heights. Tropical trees have often immense buttresses, which are plank-like out-growths from their base, and as a rule they are much less branched than the trees of our own region ; indeed, in tree-ferns, palms, and cycads, branching as a rule does not occur at all; while in higher types it is only carried out to the third order. Another peculiarity of tropical trees and climbers is the frequent occurrence of the flowers on the branches below the leaves or on the stem itself, and not with the leaves on the current year's shoot, as is the case in all our trees.

Plate XI., fig. 2, is *Bombax malabaricum,* a deciduous-leaved tree of the monsoon tropical forest, the specimen photographed occurring in a low valley in the Shan States. It shows very well the characteristic branching of tropical trees, the flowers being borne on coarse branchlets. Such trees as the elm, with its fine ramification and delicate spray, do not occur in tropical forests.

In the northern cold temperate belt, two types of forest occur, the deciduous-leaved forest, and the coniferous forest. For normal tree-growth in this belt, a rainfall of at least 20 inches yearly is necessary. In Southern Russia, the steppe is an extremely rich soil, yet trees are entirely absent, owing to the rainfall being less than 20 inches, and to the prevalence of strong, dry easterly winds. In spring and summer there are frequent showers, and the climate is thus one favourable to grass-land, and we have in consequence the treeless, grassy steppe. Similarly in the United States, rainfall is abundant at all seasons of the year in the Atlantic district, and we have here a true forest climate. Before the advent of the European, the whole country between the Mississippi and the Atlantic was covered with trees. Between the Mississippi and the Rocky Mountains there is a dry winter, followed by a moist spring and early summer—conditions favourable to grass-land. Moreover, in this region, the north winds are persistent and dry, waging war against tree-growth : as a result, we have the grassy, treeless steppes known as the prairies. Proceeding further west, a desert climate prevails on the Rocky Mountain and Sierra Nevada plateau. The Pacific slope has an abundant rainfall, and a maritime climate ; and in consequence the forests are magnificent.

The deciduous-leaved forest of colder temperate regions has at most three stages—the herbs on the ground, the shrubs, and one tier of trees, which reach a nearly uniform height. Creepers are few in species, and sparse in quantity (clematis, ivy, honey-suckle, hop). Epiphytes, at least of higher plants, are rare : indeed, only one occurs, the polypodium fern. The trees are bare, or their bark only bears lichens and algæ of no great size. This broad-leaved forest is generally mixed, when man's action does not intervene, and composed of many species, though certain ones predominate. Each species has different requirements as regards the fertility and humidity of the soil. Alders and willows flourish near water. The ash and sycamore demand a rich soil, and only occur in woods disseminated in little groups, or as isolated trees. In Europe, pure forests of deciduous broad-leaved trees are practically only formed by beech and oak. On poor soil, there may be communities of birch, which is a frugal tree, that will exist where other trees cannot find sufficient nutriment of mineral matter. The different requirements of trees have an important bearing in sylvicultural practice. There is, *e.g.*, the distinction between shade-bearers and light-demanding trees. The beech is a shade-bearer; it has a dense crown of foliage, and under-neath its shade the young beech seedlings will grow, but not those of other trees. Trees like the beech will grow crowded together in dense masses. The oak is a light-demanding tree, with a much less dense crown of foliage, and its young seedlings will not grow under cover. Moreover, when the oak reaches a certain size, the trees will not bear close crowding together, and this peculiarity necessitates different treatment of an oak-wood from that of a beech-wood. The beech is of the greatest utility as a forest tree, as its dense foliage prevents evaporation of the water of the soil, and when it falls, enriches the ground with humus. Only social trees are cultivated in extensive forests, as it is impossible to keep up pure woods of sycamore or ash on the poor soils, which are the only ones left now for the cultivation of trees. The single leader of the ash and sycamore, however, enables their seedlings to pierce their way through brushwood, thorns, briars, etc.; and is a distinct peculiarity in their favour for certain situations.

In the deciduous broad-leaved northern forest, the rich and transient spring flora is very characteristic. The shrubs become greener earlier in spring than the trees that are above them; and the ground is decked with herbs like the anemone, which go through their leafing, flowering, and fruiting before the leaves appear on the trees. The only part of these herbs that remains alive in summer is their underground stems. Certain herbs, however, do occur in these forests, which last through the summer, as they can bear shade (wood-sorrel, ferns). Other plants, as winter-green, orchids, and the enchanter's night-shade, can live in the woods, because they derive their sustenance in part from the humus.

In winter, when cold, dry winds blow, and the ground may be frozen for long periods, these broad-leaved trees are protected against transpiration of water. Their leaves fall, and this of course diminishes enormously the transpiring surface. Their stems and branches are generally protected by a layer of cork, and their buds by scales, which are resinous, or gummy, or clothed with downy hairs. The leaves, which remain only on the tree in summer, are delicate in texture, are not protected against transpiration, and stand on the twigs, so as to receive as much light as possible. They differ remarkably from such trees as the eucalyptus of hot Australia, which bear their leaves sideways on the twigs. They are also very different from the hard, leathery leaves of the Mediterranean evergreen trees. Their leaves are also much smaller than those of tropical trees. In our forests, we have a few evergreen trees, as holly, box, and arbutus: these have thick and leathery leaves, which do not transpire freely.

The coniferous forest, which is so characteristic of the northern temperate belt, has leaves, which are amply protected against transpiration in winter. A pine transpires only a tenth of the water transpired by a beech. As a rule, coniferous forests occupy colder districts than do the broad-leaved trees in the north temperate belt; they thus spread to the north, and ascend higher in the mountains. This explanation is only a general one, as mixed forests of conifers and broad-leaved species occur naturally; questions come in of soil, *e.g.,* pine woods take possession of sandy soils and heaths in regions where on other soils broad-leaved trees predominate.

Before passing on to the second part of my subject, I may lay emphasis on the point, that so far as regards the general conditions which govern tree-growth, we have in Ireland an ideal forest climate. There is a heavy rainfall, a mild climate, and an absence of cold, drying winds in winter. The strong south-westerly gales render, it is true, by their mere mechanical action of uprooting, the life of isolated trees, or narrow belts of timber, precarious. There is, however, no difficulty in establishing protective belts, chosen from such species as bear readily salt spray and strong winds; and under the lee of such belts, the more valuable kinds of trees can be successfully planted.

II. CULTIVATED FORESTS.

In wild forests nature covers the ground with trees, which, however, do not satisfy man's requirements. There are many species occurring in the wild forest, which are practically weeds, being useless as timber; and the irregular growth of even the good species makes their timber less valuable. The art of forestry consists in maintaining the good species which live in a social state, and in eliminating the worthless kinds, and inferior and diseased individuals of even the good species. Trees are grown in dense masses, because thereby tall, straight stems are obtained, which constitute valuable timber; and, at the same time, the ground is kept covered by the dense shade of the foliage of the trees, and by the layer of their dead leaves on the soil, which enrich it with humus, improve its quality by chemical and other changes, and protect it against evaporation; so that the subsoil is kept continuously wet. To improve the condition of the soil is the *main* object of the forester, just as it is of the farmer; and as the forester is deprived, on account of the expense, of extraneous fertilizing agents, he is compelled all the more, if he is wise, to utilize the great fertilizing agent of nature—the litter of leaves. The ground must be kept covered, and protected from sun and wind.

Certain species of trees—those known as shade-bearers—will grow in dense masses until they attain maturity; and with these there is no difficulty in keeping the soil covered. Others—the light-demanding kinds (the oak and larch, for example)—will not bear crowding as they reach the end of their growth; they clear themselves (as is said), and will only grow with their crowns of foliage isolated; and, in consequence, the sun and wind begin to act upon the soil, which becomes hard and bare of leaves (blown away by the wind). The soil rapidly deteriorates, with bad results to the growth of the timber on it. To obviate this condition, such forests are either mixed with (from the beginning) or under-planted (afterwards) with shade-bearing species, the object of which is to protect the soil to the end of the growth of the dominant light-demanding species.

Two types of forest are cultivated—*high forest* and *coppice.* In coppice the trees grow from shoots which spring from the stumps of felled trees; whereas in high forest the young trees are seedlings. Pure coppice is cultivated mainly for firewood or for special products, as for oak-bark, hop-poles, vine-props, etc. In *coppice with standards*, shown in Plate XII., fig. 1, the advantages of both systems are sought after. The standards are isolated large trees, as oaks or beeches, mainly regenerated by seedlings, and cut down for timber at intervals of one hundred years or so. Between the standards grows the coppice of hornbeam, lime, etc., which is cut down every twenty or thirty years, and is utilized for firewood. Coppice, owing to the lessening value of firewood and bark, is becoming a non-paying crop; whereas high forest, owing to the diminishing supply of the timber of the world, is more and more desirable; in the creation and maintenance of high forest, we are restricted to the few species that will grow socially. There are among conifers, the larch, silver fir, spruce, and pine; while of deciduous-leaved trees, the oak and beech are the most important.

The moment a forest is felled over a large area, the expenses of replanting are considerable, as the sum, however small at first, mounts up with compound interest to an enormous figure by the time that the timber is mature. Moreover, on such areas the young plants are placed in a bad condition to withstand the growth of weeds, grasses, and worthless shrubs and trees, which speedily take possession of the ground. The French have generally adopted, instead of artificial planting, the system of natural regeneration; the forest is cut down by a series of fellings, spread over a term of years, and conducted so that by the time the final cutting is made, the naturally born seedlings will be in complete possession of the soil. In the *regular system* of regeneration fellings, the forest is divided into sections, in one of which a primary cutting is done each year, the whole course of fellings being so arranged as to give a steady annual income.

This system is well carried out in the magnificent oak forest of Bercé, in France. Plate XII., fig. 2, shows a portion of the forest, with the trees about 200 years old, and thus arrived at maturity. On this section a primary regeneration felling is made; about half the trees are cut out all over the section. Those which are left standing are the finest and largest seed-bearing trees (see Plate XIII., fig. 1). The acorns germinate readily in the soil laid bare by the partial removal of the trees, and the young seedlings grow vigorously. As a rule, no operation is required to prepare the ground for the seed, though in bad spots, where grass and herbs have grown up, the ground is opened up by a slight hoeing. The seedlings gradually take possession of the ground; and during the next fifteen or twenty years a series of secondary fellings are made, which are effected wherever the seedlings are numerous. By the end of twenty years the final felling is done, and the last of the trees removed, and the seedlings now form a thick and continuous bed over the forest floor. The result of the secondary fellings is shown in Plate XIII., fig. 2. Plate XIV., fig. 1, illustrates the curious way in which the final felling is done, as the crown of the tree is lopped off by a woodman, who climbs up, and the stem thus remaining is cut down at the base afterwards. In this picture the oak in its forest form is very well shown; a tall cylindrical stem, some eighty to ninety feet in length, without a branch; the total height of the tree with the crown being about 120 feet. The crown is astonishingly small; and the unbranched trunk, all sound, useful timber, is remarkable.

Plate XIV., fig. 2, represents the young forest, after the final felling of the trees of the old forest, when the oak seedlings are in the *thicket* stage. Plate XV., fig. 1, shows the *young pole* stage, when the stems, somewhat older, have lost their lower branches, and are cleaning themselves. The trees eventually reach the stage in which they grow no more in height, but only in diameter.

When the seedlings are in a young state, *cleaning* operations are done by the woodman, who roams about the forest with a bill-hook, lopping off, wherever he finds occasion, the tops of such shrubs, or of such saplings of undesirable trees as stand above any of the young oaks, and are interfering with their growth.

Thinnings are the next operations. In France the object of thinning is never for immediate profit by the sale of the stuff cut down. Thinning is done solely with the object of favouring the best trees of the best species; all deformed, diseased, branched, unhealthy, or inferior trees of the species cultivated are removed gradually, and, at the same time, trees of undesirable species. Thinnings are directed solely against the stage in which the high trees occur; the shrubs and smaller trees which do not form part of the upper stage of the forest are never touched, as they help to cover the soil; and the preservation of the soil-cover, as explained before, is the main object of sylviculture. Thinning done severely results in the ruin of the soil, and deterioration in growth of the trees left standing, which become branched, and relatively low in stature, and so are lessened in timber value.

The value of the forest of Bercé is marvellous. The trees as they stood on one section were worth £1,000 an acre; and the value of the products of the whole forest, resultant from thinnings and fellings, averages £6 an acre.

In the *selection* system the forest is cut over extensive tracts every year, and the trees are felled either singly or in small groups of three or four, here and there, according as they become mature timber, or must be removed on account of decay or disease. In the regular system, just described, the felling is over a definite section of a certain area. However, in a well-treated selection-forest the same cultural attention, cleaning and thinning operations, are applied in the same way as in the other system, only over greater areas less intensively. The selection system is in vogue in mountainous districts, where natural regeneration on account of climate or soil is difficult, and where hurricanes are frequent, and it is not advisable to make any great openings in the forest mass by fellings.

The Vosges is a mountainous tract of France, where the soil is almost barren, consisting of 95 per cent. of pure silica with no lime, and the merest trace of phosphates. With such a soil, agriculture and pasture are impossible in the Vosges, except in the valleys; and yet, over eighty-five per cent. of the whole district, the mountains are covered by dense forests, composed of silver fir, pure, or mixed with beech or spruce. To give one example of the value of these forests, the 2,400 acres belonging to the hospitals of Nancy, situated at an average height of 3,000 feet, yield an annual income by the sale of timber of £4,000 net.

The silver fir is a pronounced shade-bearer, and its young seedlings spring up under the cover of the parent trees, and retain their vitality for a long time, although, of course, they will not grow vigorously until they are uncovered, and exposed to the light. The silver fir only succeeds in a climate which is very humid, and not too cold; and in nature it occurs as a tree of the lower parts of the mountains of central Europe. Both the selection and regular systems are in vogue with silver-fir forests. Plate XV., fig. 2, is a general view of a silver-fir forest in the Vosges.

At a considerable altitude the silver fir is difficult to cultivate pure, on account of the uncertainty of natural regeneration; and in such cases spruce is mixed with it. Young seedlings may also be introduced artificially from the lower levels.

In the Jura, which is of limestone formation, equally remarkable results are obtained. To quote one example: on the small chain of Risoux, there is a forest of spruce, belonging to several neighbouring communes, which is 6,500 acres in area, at 4,000 feet elevation; and it yields a net yearly income of ten shillings an acre. Here the conditions of soil and climate are so difficult—as the ground is almost pure rock, and cold, drying winds prevail in winter—that in most parts of this forest the young seedling spruces find no place to take root but on the decaying stumps of the felled trees, and in the crevices of the rocks, where falling leaves have decayed, and made pockets of humus. Here, of course, the selection system is adopted; no extensive fellings are ever made, where the hurricanes might enter and cause widespread devastation. Where young seedlings are found, a few trees over them are cut down to give them light, and the chance to grow up into big trees; and in this way the older trees are taken out as it were one by one, being replaced by the natural seedlings. The timber of the spruce of these high altitudes is extremely valuable, as the trees grow slowly; for the rule with conifers is that the slower the growth the better the wood produced. Hence follow the possibility and desirability of cultivating conifers in mountainous districts, as the slowness in growth is made up for by the improvement in the quality of the timber.

Plate XVI., fig. 1, represents a mixed forest of spruce and silver fir. Plate XVI., fig. 2, is interesting, as illustrating the importance of humidity of the subsoil. It is a spruce forest in the mountains, through which a road passes horizontally (from front to back in the picture). The road acts as a drain; as a result, the lower part of the wood (on the left of the picture) shows the trees growing densely and luxuriantly. The part of the forest immediately above the road (and drained by it) has the trees growing much less crowded, and they are not flourishing.

In the mountains of Central Europe, the natural succession of conifers is—the silver fir at low altitudes; the spruce higher up; the larch highest of all, and forming the timber line in many localities.

Plate XVII., fig. 1, shows the spruce in the Jura at 5,000 feet, where the Alpine grass-land begins. We see that the trees are isolated, the scene becoming park-like in character; and with the grass are associated plants like the white hellebore and the yellow gentian.

The larch, though extensively cultivated in this country, is an exotic, and is far removed from its natural conditions of growth. Its wonderful success, now rendered less certain by the disastrous disease which afflicts it, is an encouragement to seek in some other exotic conifer a tree that will replace it. The larch is an Alpine tree in central Europe, only descending to the plain in the cold and dry climate of Northern Russia. Plate XVII., fig. 2, shows a regular forest of larch at a high elevation, and exhibits very well how the tree—a light-demanding species—grows in its natural situation isolatedly, when it has attained a certain size. Such a forest presents a marked contrast to the dense mass of a forest of a typical shade-bearing tree like the silver fir.

The mountain pine, a very distinct species, not to be confused with the common pine or Scotch fir, occurs naturally in two kinds of situation in the mountains of central Europe, either in bogs or on rocky places, ascending, in the latter case, even higher than the larch. Plate XVIII., fig. 1, represents the species growing on a bog in the Jura, near Pontarlier, at 4,000 feet elevation. It is evidently a tree of some value for high mountain bogs; but at lower altitudes, the common pine is more suitable for mountain bogs, and does very well at Longemer, in the Vosges, in a bog, to which some manure and the ashes obtained by burning the heather and other shrubs have been added. Plate XVIII., fig. 2, shows the mountain pine, at 4,800 to 6,000 feet on the southern slopes of Mount Ventoux. It is the only tree which will cover the soil at such elevations. Plate XIX., fig. 1, represents the continuation of the same forest, higher up towards the timber line; and the trees, as they ascend, become smaller and smaller; finally, they are quite stunted and markedly isolated. On these high mountains, for protection against land-slips, &c., the French make artificial plantations of this species, which succeed on the most difficult and rocky slopes. Such plantations are part of the general works carried on by the French foresters on the high mountains, which are being gradually afforested to prevent land-slips, disastrous floods, and other calamities, which are the concomitants of bare Alpine mountains. The improvement on the mountain pastures is another work which is carried out by the foresters; drainage, irrigation, and periods of closure to cattle, are the chief means adopted for this end.

The protection of the land against the encroachment of the sea-sands, on certain parts of the coast, is another section of the forester's work; and in the Landes, the fixing of the dunes has gone on in conjunction with the afforestation of tracts that were formerly deserts. Years ago the Landes was a territory almost quite barren, inhabited by only a few shepherds on stilts, who herded scanty flocks of sheep, there being no towns, or villages, or cultivation. This vast territory was a series of sand-hills, built up by sand blowing in from the sea in the course of ages; and between the chains of sand-hills were marshes and lagoons. The entire country was unhealthy, malarious, poor, and miserable. The afforestation begun eighty years ago has resulted in the creation of the great forest of maritime pine, covering 1,500,000 acres (the greatest forest in Western Europe); and the whole territory is now healthy, full of villages and industries, and inhabited by a comfortable population.

From Bordeaux to Bayonne, by the beginning of the nineteenth century the sea-sand drifting in had covered the country with a series of dunes, rising to 250 feet high. The first remedial step was to erect along the coast a protecting wall; this great wall has been built by the foresters, not by any feat of engineering force (costly, laborious, withal inefficient), but by enlisting the ordinary forces of nature, the wind and plant-growth. To create this wall (and the work has often to be renewed), about one hundred yards from the sea, a continuous line of paling is put down, consisting of stout planks, standing about a yard above the ground, with short intervals between them, through which the sand drifts and serves as a backing. As the sand-bank rises around the paling, the planks are lifted up a few feet at a time; and a rough wattled fence is also run behind the paling, which is renewed as it becomes covered. Gradually the sand-hill is thus raised, till it is about 60 feet high; and it is then fixed by plantation of marrem grass (*Psamma arenaria*). It constitutes the littoral dune, and is a great bank of sand, the wall that protects the coast. By judicious planting, and transplanting, and thinning of the grass, the dune is made to assume a definite slope, that of maximum stability. Behind the littoral dune the land is planted with a mixture of seed of maritime pine, furze, and broom; and in this way the forest of maritime pine has been created. The trees are tapped for resin, which is refined into rosin and turpentine; and the wood of mature trees is used for pit props, railway sleepers, etc.

Plate XIX., fig. 2, shows women planting marrem grass on the dune. Plate XX., fig. 1, represents the tapping of the resin.

Further south, near Bayonne, the maritime pine is accompanied by the cork oak, which is here at its northern limit. The naturally grown cork is of no value except for the rudest purposes. When the trees attain a certain age, this naturally grown cork is removed down to the cork-forming layer, which is at some distance in the interior. This genetic layer forms new bark, which grows in regular uniform layers, and constitutes the ordinary cork of commerce. A tree of 8 inches diameter in the forest near Bayonne will yield cork to the value of about six shillings; and there may be forty trees to the acre. Besides the cork trees, there are the accompanying maritime pines, with their product of timber and resin. Plate XIX., fig. 2, represents an oak from which the virgin cork has been stripped.

In the preceding I have drawn all my illustrations of cultivated forests from France, where there is an astonishing variety, dependent upon the varied nature of the soil, altitude, and climate of that country. The French are adepts at the economical use of the forces of nature; and their modern forestry appears to me to be due in large measure to the necessity under which the French have laboured, of carrying on their forests at a minimum of expense. Forestry to succeed in Ireland must depend upon a similar patient observation of nature, and careful utilization of the forces which she puts at our disposal.

[NOTE.—For permission to reproduce figs. 8, 9, 10, 12, and 13, I am indebted to Professor Fron, of the Forest School at Les Barres.]

1.

2.

2.

1.

2.

1.

1

2.

1.

2

1.

2.

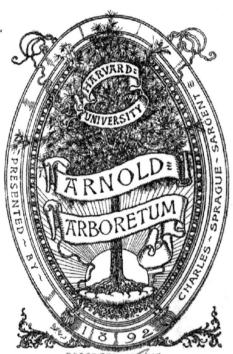

THE

ECONOMIC PROCEEDINGS OF THE ROYAL DUBLIN SOCIETY

VOLUME I, PART V, No. VI.

FORESTS, WILD AND CULTIVATED

BY

AUGUSTINE HENRY, M.A.
F.L.S., etc.

PLATES III. to XV.

PLATE XV.

1.

Plate XVII.

1.

1.

2.

1.

2

1.

2.

1.

2.

PLATE XVII.

1.

2.

Plate XVIII.

1.

2.

2.

1.

1.

2.

CPSIA information can be obtained at www.ICGtesting.com
Printed in the USA
LVOW112025200712

290934LV00012B/44/P

9 781286 292754